ROME & ROMANS

Heather Amery and Patricia Vanags
Edited by Philippa Wingate

Designed by Michele Busby and John Jamieson
Series designer: Russell Punter

Illustrated by Stephen Cartwright

Contents

2	Going back in time	16	Games and races
3	The people you will meet	18	Building in the city
4	The road to Rome	20	Petronius gives a feast
6	In the streets of Rome	22	Summer on the farm
8	Petronius at home	24	Marcus joins the army
10	Going to school	26	Attack!
12	Going shopping	28	The Roman empire
14	At the baths	30	The story of Rome
		32	Index

GOING BACK IN TIME

To visit Ancient Rome, you would have to travel back in time nearly 2,000 years. With your magic time travel helmet, this journey will only take a few seconds.

In museums you will find pieces of Roman furniture, and see pictures of Roman people at work or play. But museums can't show you everything you want to see.

So put on your magic helmet, set the Date Dial to "AD100" (which means 100 years after Jesus was born), and the Place Indicator to "Italy".

1. THE TIME HELMET

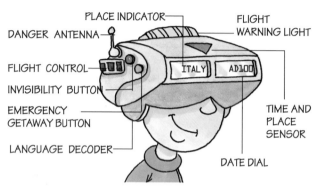

PLACE INDICATOR
DANGER ANTENNA
FLIGHT WARNING LIGHT
FLIGHT CONTROL
INVISIBILITY BUTTON
ITALY AD100
EMERGENCY GETAWAY BUTTON
TIME AND PLACE SENSOR
LANGUAGE DECODER
DATE DIAL

This is your magic time travel helmet. It has lots of useful buttons, for understanding foreign languages, flying, being invisible, and making a quick escape back home.

2. PICK A DESTINATION

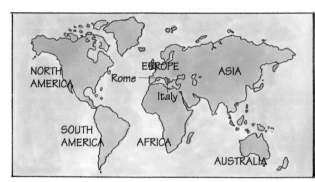

NORTH AMERICA
EUROPE
Rome
ASIA
Italy
SOUTH AMERICA
AFRICA
AUSTRALIA

Today, you are going to Rome, which is in southern Europe. Below are a few stop-off points to give you an idea of how different things look when you travel back 2,000 years in time.

3. GO!

1940

This is northwest Europe in 1940. Things have not changed much, but notice the plane and the radio. Most families don't have TVs.

1900

After a jump of 40 years, things have changed a lot. There is a strange-looking telephone, and the woman is wearing a long skirt.

1600

Back another 300 years and you will find the room is lit by candles, and there is a big log fire in the fireplace. Notice the small window with little panes of glass.

1200

Now we are in the days when some people lived in big, cold castles. There is no chimney for the fire, and no glass in the windows. Next stop Ancient Rome!

THE PEOPLE YOU WILL MEET

Everyone you will meet in this book lives in the city of Rome, which is in the country now called Italy. Most of the people who live in and around Rome are known as Romans. Only slaves and foreign visitors are not called Romans.

You will come across both rich and poor people in this book, and you will be able to see how different their lives are.

Roman men are called citizens. There are three main types of citizens: noblemen, businessmen and ordinary people, such as farmers, store keepers and craftsmen.

Poor store keepers and craftsmen are often men who have been set free from slavery by their masters.

Wealthy people have pleasant, easy lives, because they have lots of slaves to do all the work.

Slaves are mostly captured foreigners, who are bought at slave markets. If they run away, they are beaten or put to death.

PETRONIUS AND HIS FAMILY

The main people you will meet are a nobleman named Petronius, his wife, Livia, and their family.

Petronius is a rich man who lives in a large house in Rome. He is a lawyer and an important official in the government. Livia looks after the house, and has many slaves to help her.

MARCUS

Marcus is 16 and training to be a soldier. Like all children, he has to obey his father and ask permission before he does anything.

CORNELIA

Cornelia is the eldest daughter. She is 14 years old and engaged to a young nobleman. Until her wedding, she will live at home.

MARIUS

Marius is 15 years old. He is learning about his father's business. When he is older, he will serve in the army for a while, like Marcus.

CLAUDIA

Claudia is 12 and lives at home. She has finished school. Now her mother is teaching her to spin and weave. A tutor gives her music lessons.

CAIUS

Caius, the youngest, is eight and goes to school. He doesn't like the schoolmaster and would rather play all day.

AUNT ANTONIA

Petronius's sister Antonia and her children live with the family. Her husband was killed while he was fighting with the army.

SESTIUS

Sestius is Petronius's cousin. He is visiting the family to ask for Petronius's help with some legal business.

PERICLES

Pericles is Petronius's secretary. He used to be a slave, but he works so well that Petronius has given him his freedom.

THE ROAD TO ROME

The year is AD100, and your time travel helmet has brought you to Italy. You are hovering above a road just outside Rome.

Rome is the biggest city in Europe. Only 700 years before your visit, it was just a village of wooden huts built on one of seven hills. Gradually, the city grew and now there are stone houses, temples and public buildings built on all of the seven hills.

Today, there are lots of people on the road to Rome.

PIPELINE, CALLED AN AQUEDUCT, RIES FRESH WATER TO ROME.

THE CITY OF ROME

RUIT TREES

CARTS CARRY FRESH FOOD TO THE CITY.

BARGES CARRY GRAIN FROM AFRICA AND EGYPT INTO ROME.

THIS FARMER IS PLOUGHING HIS FIELD BEFORE SOWING A SPRING CROP.

THE TIBER RIVER

FISHERMEN

IN THE STREETS OF ROME

The Romans rule over an empire which is made up of the many lands they have conquered. Rome is the capital of this empire.

It is a splendid city, with huge palaces, beautiful houses, bathhouses and arches. Many of the finest buildings shine in the sun because they are covered with thin slabs of marble.

At the time of your journey, the Romans are so powerful that Rome doesn't need walls to protect it from enemies.

In the middle of the city are several open squares called forums. They were built at different times by different Roman emperors.

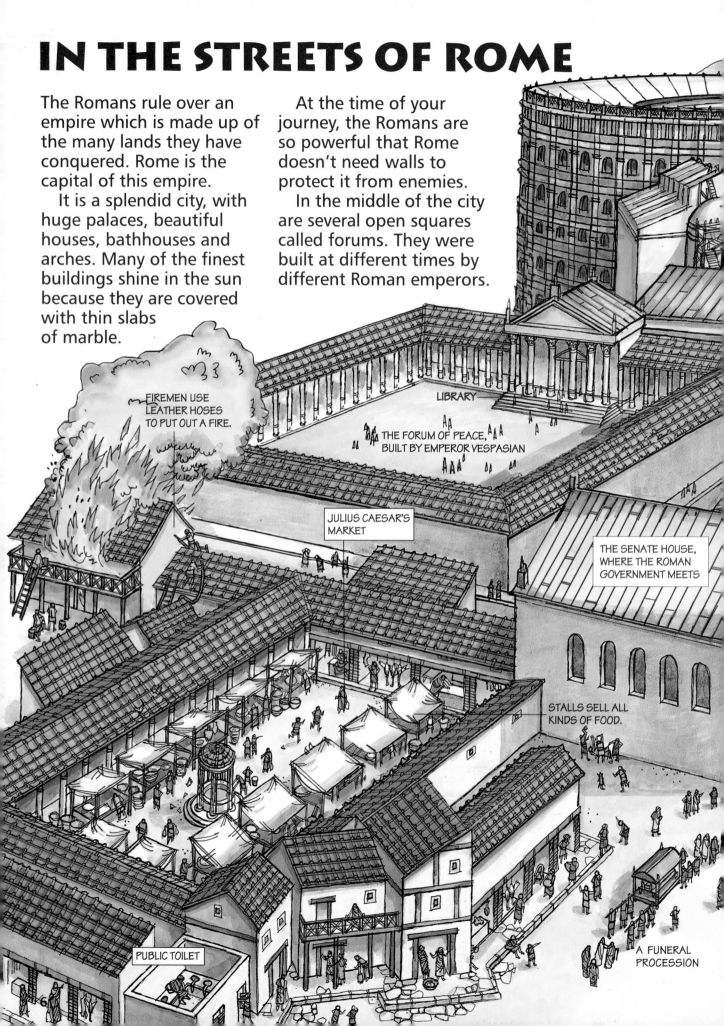

FIREMEN USE LEATHER HOSES TO PUT OUT A FIRE.

LIBRARY

THE FORUM OF PEACE, BUILT BY EMPEROR VESPASIAN

JULIUS CAESAR'S MARKET

THE SENATE HOUSE, WHERE THE ROMAN GOVERNMENT MEETS

STALLS SELL ALL KINDS OF FOOD.

PUBLIC TOILET

A FUNERAL PROCESSION

A HUGE ARENA
CALLED THE COLOSSEUM

THE PALACE WHERE THE
ROMAN EMPEROR LIVES

THE BASILICA
AEMILIA,
WHERE MEN DO
BUSINESS

TEMPLE OF THE VESTALS,
WHERE PRIESTESSES
KEEP A FIRE BURNING
ALL THE TIME

TEMPLE
OF CAESAR

THESE SOLDIERS ARE MARCHING
THROUGH THE CITY TO CELEBRATE
WINNING A BATTLE.

THIS PLATFORM IS CALLED
THE NEW ROSTRA. IT IS USED
BY PUBLIC SPEAKERS.

HIEF

PETRONIUS AT HOME

This is where Petronius lives. He has a very large and comfortable house because he is wealthy and important.

The house has high walls and small windows to prevent thieves from getting in. The floors are made of stone. In the middle of the house there is a large hall which has an open roof.

Petronius is the master of his household and everyone has to obey him. But he is kind, and treats his slaves and servants well. When he wants new slaves, he buys them at a slave market.

This morning, Petronius busy working in his office with his secretary, Pericles A man has come to ask if he can borrow a large sur of money. Marius watche his father doing business.

IN A BEDROOM, LIVIA AND CORNELIA ARE PREPARING TO GO OUT TO VISIT FRIENDS.

SERVANTS HELP LIVIA.

DOOR-KEEPERS PROTECT THE HOUSE, KEEPING WATCH FOR THIEVES.

KITCHEN

THIS MAN HAS COME TO BORROW SOME MONEY FROM PETRONIUS.

SERVANT'S ROOM

TOILET

A LEAD PIPE BRINGS WATER INTO THE HOUSE.

A DRAIN CARRIES AWAY DIRTY WATER.

Petronius sees important visitors at once. Less important people often have to wait in the street.

When his business is done, Petronius may visit friends, or go to the law courts to take care of legal matters.

PUTTING ON A TOGA

Before he sees visitors, Petronius puts on a robe which is known as a toga. A slave carefully arranges the folds of heavy material for him.

Only men who are citizens of Rome are allowed to wear togas.

TOGA

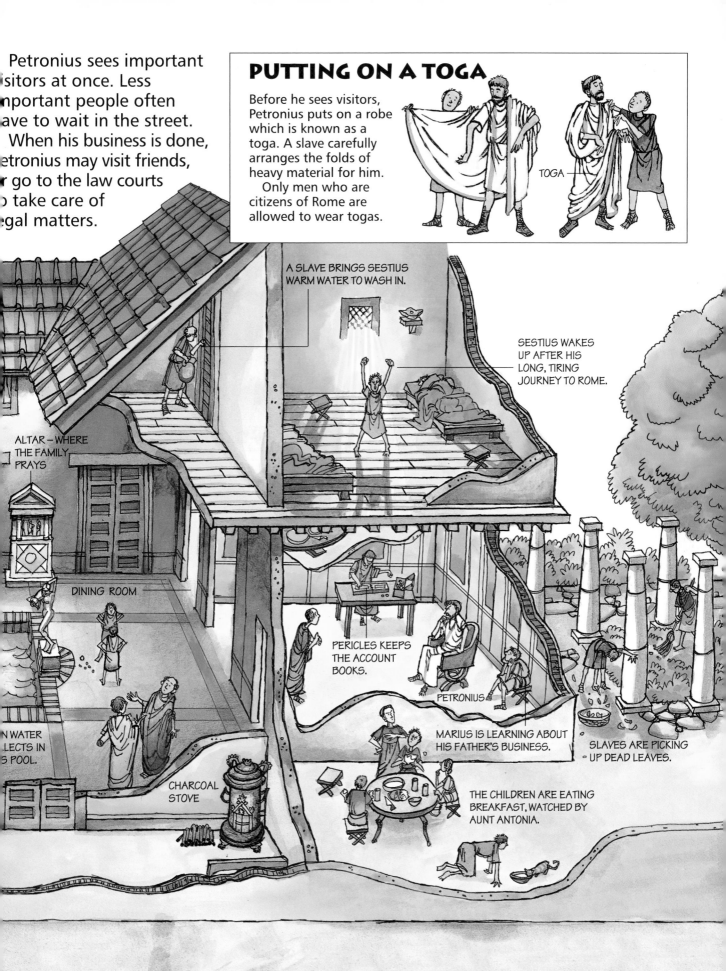

A SLAVE BRINGS SESTIUS WARM WATER TO WASH IN.

SESTIUS WAKES UP AFTER HIS LONG, TIRING JOURNEY TO ROME.

ALTAR – WHERE THE FAMILY PRAYS

DINING ROOM

PERICLES KEEPS THE ACCOUNT BOOKS.

PETRONIUS

N WATER LECTS IN S POOL.

CHARCOAL STOVE

MARIUS IS LEARNING ABOUT HIS FATHER'S BUSINESS.

SLAVES ARE PICKING UP DEAD LEAVES.

THE CHILDREN ARE EATING BREAKFAST, WATCHED BY AUNT ANTONIA.

GOING TO SCHOOL

Caius is on his way to school. Lessons begin so early in the morning that it is still dark, and Caius carries a torch to light his way.

Roman families pay schoolmasters to teach their children. The children of very wealthy families are taught at home by tutors.

Sometimes tutors who are set free from slavery start up their own schools.

FAMILIES LIVE IN THE ROOMS ABOVE THE STORES AND SCHOOLS.

A BAKER GETS UP EARLY TO SELL BREAD TO THE CHILDREN.

CAIUS LIGHTS HIS WAY TO SCHOOL WITH A TORCH.

OIL LAMP

A FAMOUS WRITER

THIS BOY FORGOT HIS LESSON.

THIS SLAVE IS TAKING A BOY TO SCHOOL.

OLDER BOYS LEARN GREEK AND LATIN, GEOMETRY AND HISTORY.

GAMES

School finishes early in the afternoon, so there is plenty of time for the children to play games.

HOOPS ARE FUN FOR ROLLING AND JUMPING THROUGH.

THESE GIRLS ARE PLAYING A GAME CALLED JACKS, WITH FIVE SMALL BONES AND A BALL.

WOODEN SWORDS

STICK AND BALL GAMES

10

WRITING

WAX TABLETS

SCROLL

PEN AND INK

Schoolchildren write on boards spread with wax. They scratch words or sums in the wax with pointed sticks. They can erase mistakes with the flat end of the stick.

Roman books are rolls of paper, called scrolls. They are written by hand. Each end of the roll is stuck to a rod. Readers have to unroll the paper to see each page.

People write on scrolls with pens made of small reeds or of copper. They use ink made from a mixture of soot, a kind of tar called pitch, and black ink from an octopus.

A FAMOUS THINKER

SCHOOL-MASTER

A NAUGHTY BOY DRAWING ON A WALL.

A BOY RECITING A POEM HE HAS LEARNED.

THIS IS A SCHOOL FOR YOUNG CHILDREN. THEY LEARN TO READ AND WRITE AND DO SIMPLE MATHEMATICS.

JAVELINS

CHILDREN LEARN TO SWIM WITH BAMBOO FLOATS.

FLOAT

BOYS RACING THEIR CARTS PRETEND TO BE REAL CHARIOTEERS.

GOING SHOPPING

Petronius and Livia have gone shopping in Rome's narrow, dusty streets. There are weavers, silversmiths and shoemakers. At the bakery below, people are baking bread for the customers.

Rich people only go shopping for their clothes, jewels and other expensive things. They send their servants or slaves to buy food and wine.

Every day, fresh food is sold in the city at open-air markets. Very early in the morning, noisy wooden carts bring the goods into Rome from farms outside.

WHEAT

LOAVES IN THE OVEN

STONE MILL

FLOUR

DOUGH

AT THE BAKERY, WHEAT IS GROUND INTO FLOUR. IT IS MIXED INTO DOUGH, AND BAKED IN THE OVEN.

CUSTOMERS

People stop in the streets to gossip and hear the latest news of the wars and the empire.

Livia and Petronius are buying material from a cloth merchant. Livia wants a new tunic to wear at a feast.

A pharmacist makes ointments from herbs, flowers and seeds. People who are sick also buy magic spells.

CLEANING CLOTHES

Rich Romans have their togas cleaned by men called fullers. The togas are spread on frames and bleached white.

Then the fullers put the togas in tubs of water and a special clay. They tread on them to get all the dirt out.

The clothes are dried and folded, and then put in a big press to flatten them. The Romans do not have irons.

Slaves collect their masters' clean clothes. They have to make sure the work has been done well before paying.

HE MARKET

day is a market day. Stalls are
t up in a city square. They sell
it and vegetables, meat and
h. Musicians play to earn a
w coins from
e crowd.

s customer is a slave. She is
osing a goose to take home and
k for a special feast tonight.

A butcher chops up a pig's head in his shop. Only rich people can afford meat every day.

This woman is selling hot food for people to eat at home. Many houses do not have stoves for cooking.

AT THE BATHS

When Petronius has finished his work, he goes to the public bathhouse. There are lots of baths in Rome and they cost very little to use. Very few people have baths in their homes.

The baths are not just places for washing. They are good places to go to meet friends or do business. Some people go there to do exercises, walk in the gardens or read quietly.

PEOPLE LEAVE THEIR CLOTHES ON SHELVES IN THE CHANGING ROOM

SOME PEOPLE LIVE IN THESE APARTMENTS.

COLD BATH FOR COOLING DOWN AND SWIMMING

CAKE SELLER

PEOPLE ENJOY WALKING IN THE GARDEN.

WRESTLERS

WARM BATH, FOR COOLING DOWN AFTER THE HOT BATH OR THE STEAM ROOM

VERY HOT BATH, WHERE EVERYONE SWEATS A LOT

THIS MAN IS BEING MASSAGED AND RUBBED WITH OIL IN A PRIVATE ROOM.

BATHERS SCRAPE THEMSELVES CLEAN WITH SPECIAL SCRAPERS. THEY DON'T USE SOAP.

THE HOTTEST ROOM IS HEATED BY STEAM.

THIS THIEF IS STEALING A TUNIC.

HOLLOW FLOOR

WATER TANK

HOT AIR FLOWS THROUGH TUNNELS UNDER THE FLOOR AND HEATS THE BATHS. THIS SYSTEM IS CALLED A HYPOCAUST.

WATER FLOWS ALONG AQUEDUCTS AND UNDERGROUND PIPES FROM OUTSIDE THE CITY.

A SLAVE CARRYING HIS MASTER'S THINGS

A SLAVE STOKES THE FIRE TO HEAT WATER FOR THE BATHS.

15

GAMES AND RACES

At festival time and on public holidays, Petronius takes his family to race tracks or arenas to be entertained.

In arenas, prisoners and criminals are put to death. Some are attacked by wild animals, others have to fight gladiators. Gladiators are men who have been sentenced to death. They train at special schools to fight and die bravely.

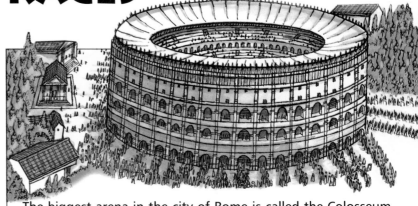

The biggest arena in the city of Rome is called the Colosseum. It is enormous and can seat up to 50,000 people.

WILD ANIMALS FROM ALL OVER THE EMPIRE ARE BROUGHT TO FIGHT.

THIS LION WAS CAPTURED IN NORTH AFRICA.

GLADIATOR CONTESTS

To make the fights more exciting, gladiators use a variety of weapons. This man has a net. He is dodging a sharp sword.

When he gets a chance, he flings his net over his opponent. He tries to tangle him up in it and stab him with a fisherman's spear.

The wounded man begs for mercy. If the crowd gives a "thumbs up" sign, he will live. A "thumbs down" means he must be killed.

THE CIRCUS

Chariot races are held at a large track called the Circus. The horses race around the track seven times. Everyone shouts with excitement as the chariots speed past. The drivers are in four different teams – reds, greens, blues and whites. The winning driver is given a purse full of gold and treated like a hero.

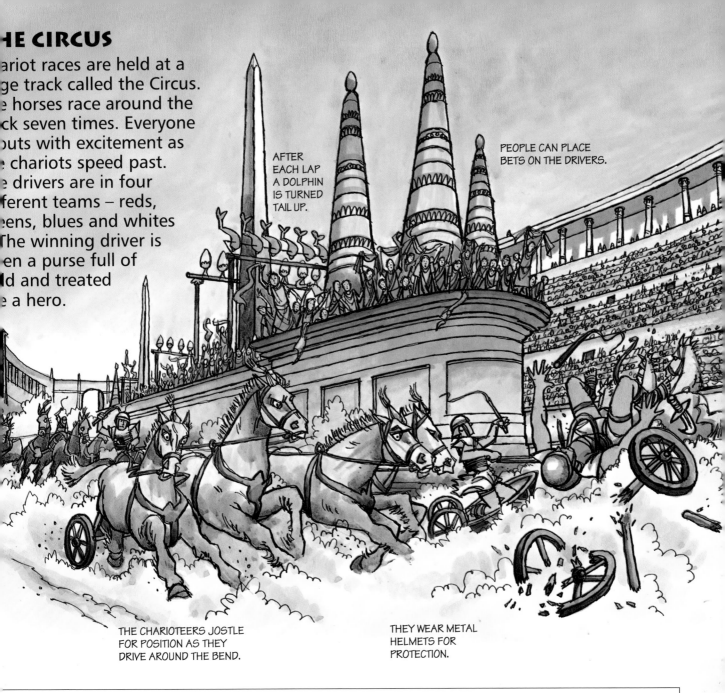

AFTER EACH LAP A DOLPHIN IS TURNED TAIL UP.

PEOPLE CAN PLACE BETS ON THE DRIVERS.

THE CHARIOTEERS JOSTLE FOR POSITION AS THEY DRIVE AROUND THE BEND.

THEY WEAR METAL HELMETS FOR PROTECTION.

A CHARIOT RACE

At the beginning of a race, the charioteers wait at the starting line. Each man leans forward to help balance the light chariot, which is made of wood and leather.

A trumpet sounds, the starter drops his white flag, and they are off. The reins are tied around the charioteers' waists, so they can lean back and whip their horses.

If a chariot crashes or a horse stumbles, the driver pulls out his dagger. He quickly cuts the reins to stop himself from being dragged along the ground by the horses.

17

BUILDING IN THE CITY

Rome is always filled with the sound of building. Old houses are pulled down, and new and bigger ones are put up in their places.

Today, some craftsmen are constructing a huge new aqueduct, while others are building a house for a wealthy Roman merchant.

THIS IS A NEW AQUEDUCT
WILL CARRY WATER TO BA
AND FOUNTAINS IN THE C

STONE BLOCKS

RUBBLE IS TAKEN AWAY.

THIS ARTIST IS PAINTING A PICTURE CALLED A MURAL ON WET PLASTER.

THIS MAN IS BUILDING A WALL OF BRICKS MADE OF BAKED CLAY.

THIS MAN IS PLASTERING A NEW WALL.

ASSISTANT

TILES

THESE MEN ARE MAKING A FLOOR OUT OF PIECES OF MARBLE.

18

CARVING A TOMBSTONE

This man is carving a tombstone. Even poor people save up to buy tombstones.

He is carving a portrait of the dead man, whose name was P. Licinius Philonicus.

The mason has carved pictures of tools on the stone to show that the man made coins.

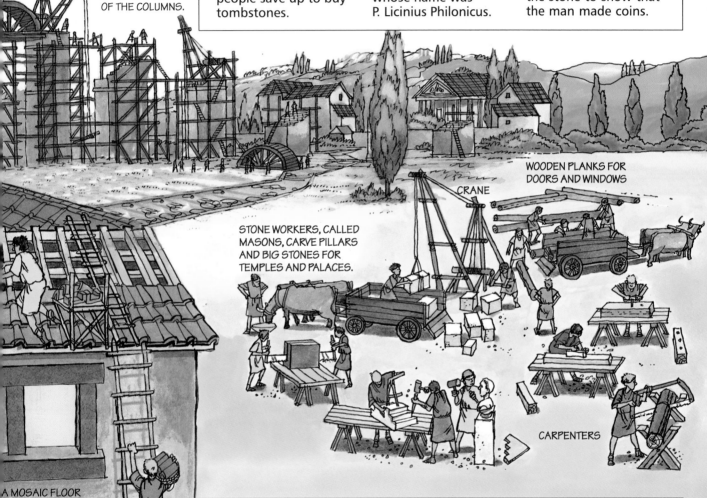

S SCAFFOLDING WILL TAKEN AWAY WHEN E ARCH IS COMPLETE.

A CRANE LIFTS HEAVY STONES UP TO THE TOPS OF THE COLUMNS.

STONE WORKERS, CALLED MASONS, CARVE PILLARS AND BIG STONES FOR TEMPLES AND PALACES.

CRANE

WOODEN PLANKS FOR DOORS AND WINDOWS

CARPENTERS

A MOSAIC FLOOR IS BEING LAID IN THIS ROOM.

WET PLASTER

HOW TO MAKE A MOSAIC

GLASS AND STONE

WET PLASTER

A craftsman spreads wet plaster over a small patch of the floor. Then he smooths it down.

He presses little squares of glass or stone into the plaster. Little by little, he makes up a picture.

When the picture is finished, he rubs more plaster all over it to fill in the small gaps between the squares.

PETRONIUS GIVES A FEAST

Tonight, Petronius has asked some friends to dinner. All day, his servants and slaves have been hard at work in the kitchen preparing delicious food.

The guests are lying on couches and eating the food with their fingers. Petronius's servants make sure that they all have plenty of wine to drink.

Servants can't afford to eat fish or meat. Instead, they have dull food, such porridge made from whe Sometimes, Petronius hol a special feast for them.

SLAVES CARRY A LADY TO THE FEAST IN A BOX CALLED A LITTER.

THIS GUEST IS LATE. THE ROMANS ONLY HAVE SUN DIALS AND HOUR GLASSES, SO IT'S HARD TO BE ON TIME.

ROASTING MEAT OVER A FIRE

VEGETABLES AND SAUCES ARE COOKED ON A STOVE.

THE KITCHEN IS HOT, DARK, DIRTY AND VERY BUSY.

TWO SLAVES PLAY DICE WH WAITING FOR THEIR MASTE WHO IS ONE OF THE GUEST

COOKING

HERBS
WINE
FISH
HONEY   PEPPER

The head cook is making sauce for a meat dish. He pounds up the insides of fish with some herbs, spices, wine and honey.

BEANS
PEAS
MARROWS   ONIONS
LETTUCE

Two slaves chop up beans, onions, asparagus, lettuce and garlic. The vegetables will be eaten raw for the first course.

SNAILS
OYSTERS

Live snails left in milk for two days have grown fat. One slave takes them out of their shells, while another slave opens oysters.

N THE DINING ROOM

LESS IMPORTANT GUESTS EAT CHEAPER FOOD AT THIS TABLE.

OIL LAMP

THIS IS THE CHIEF GUEST. HE IS BUSY DICTATING LETTERS TO HIS SECRETARY WHILE HE EATS.

A PIPE

THIS MAN IS TELLING A STORY ABOUT HIS RECENT TRIP TO BRITAIN.

THIS SLAVE IS POURING PETRONIUS SOME WINE.

THIS MAN IS PLAYING A CITHERA.

THE MOST IMPORTANT GUESTS SIT AT THE MAIN TABLE AND HAVE THE NICEST FOOD.

GUESTS WASH THEIR HANDS BETWEEN COURSES.

OET WAITS TO ITE POEMS.

FIRST COURSE

OIL AND EGG SAUCE

STUFFED DORMICE

PEACOCKS' EGGS

The first course is a dish of stuffed and cooked dormice, stuffed olives and prunes, and peacocks' eggs with a sauce.

MAIN COURSE

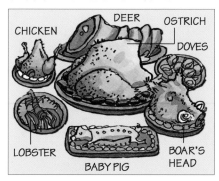

DEER

OSTRICH

CHICKEN

DOVES

LOBSTER

BABY PIG

BOAR'S HEAD

Boiled and roasted meat is served for the second course. It is sliced by the slaves, as the guests don't have any knives or forks.

THIRD COURSE

FRUIT

HONEY CAKES

STUFFED DATES

The last course is fruit, dates and cakes sweetened with honey. After this, the guests drink a toast to each other's health.

SUMMER ON THE FARM

During the summer, Rome is a very hot and smelly place. So Petronius has decided to take his family and servants to the countryside for a few weeks. He owns a big house, called a villa, which stands in the middle of his farmland.

September is a very busy time on the farm. Grapes and olives have to be picked and made into wine and oil. All kinds of food have to be collected and stored, so they can be eaten during the winter.

THE WHEAT STUBBLE IS BEING BURNED.

MEN KNOCKING OLIVES OFF THE TREES

APPLE TREES

STABLES

OIL AND WINE ARE STORED IN POTTERY JARS.

LOOM

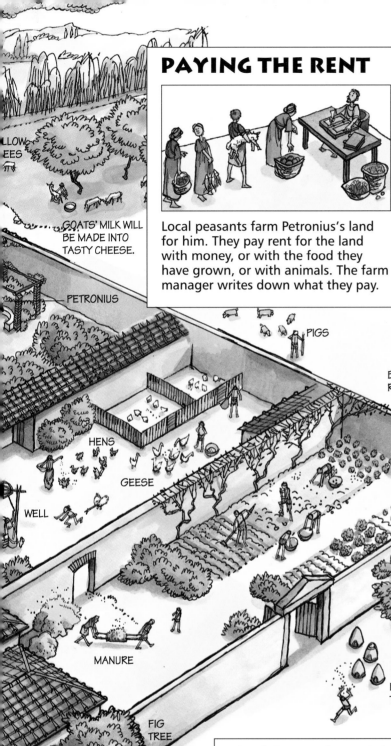

PAYING THE RENT

Local peasants farm Petronius's land for him. They pay rent for the land with money, or with the food they have grown, or with animals. The farm manager writes down what they pay.

PRESSING OLIVES

When the olives have been harvested, they are put into a screw press. Workers wind the handles to squash the olives and squeeze out the oil.

LLOW
EES

GOATS' MILK WILL BE MADE INTO TASTY CHEESE.

PETRONIUS

PIGS

BUNCHES OF RIPE GRAPES

HENS

GEESE

WELL

MANURE

BEEHIVES MADE OF THIN, WOVEN TWIGS

GRAPEVINES

FIG TREE

A SLAVE IS WEAVING BASKETS OUT OF STICKS CUT FROM THE WILLOW TREES BY THE RIVER.

MAKING WINE

Grapes are poured into a stone trough. Men tread on them to squash out the juice. They hold sticks to stop them from slipping over on the mushy grape skins.

The grape skins are then put into a press to squeeze out the rest of the juice. The juice is put into big jars. It bubbles and foams as it turns into wine.

MARCUS JOINS THE ARMY

Petronius's son Marcus has joined the Roman army, and has been sent to a camp with other new recruits. While he is at the camp, Marcus will be taught all the things soldiers have to know when fighting Rome's enemies.

Marcus and the other new soldiers have their names written down in the army record book. They have to swear an oath and promise to be loyal to the emperor. They will swear this oath again every year.

LIFE IN THE CAMP

Marcus is measured by an army tailor who will make his uniform. Marcus has to wear a tunic, and a breast plate made of metal and leather.

Next, he tries on several bronze helmets to find one which is the right size. The helmets are lined with leather to protect soldiers' heads.

The training will make the new recruits strong and good at fightir They start with marching twice a c carrying spears and heavy packs.

Marcus learns to fight by running at a target with a wooden sword. Sometimes, he and the other boys fight each other with swords and spears in mock battles.

Horse riding is fun, but everyone laughs when Marcus falls off. There are no stirrups for his feet, so it is hard to balance in the saddle while carrying a heavy shield.

The recruits learn to lock their shiel together to make a formation call a "tortoise". This will protect then from enemy arrows and stones, bu it is not easy for beginners.

24

SOLDIERS AT WORK

The recruits learn how to make a camp out of turf and wooden stakes. This will be useful when they are marching through enemy territory.

They learn how to use mallets and chisels to cut and shape stones. They are also taught how to bake clay roof tiles in an oven.

To build roads, they dig wide ditches and fill them with stones. Flat stones go on top. The roads slope down on each side so water runs off them.

THE ARMY CAMP

The army camp is huge, and it is surrounded by strong stone walls. Outside the walls, a little town has been built. There are houses and market stalls, and people farm the land.

They sell the food they grow and the clothes they make to the troops. Sometimes the soldiers' families come to live outside the camp.

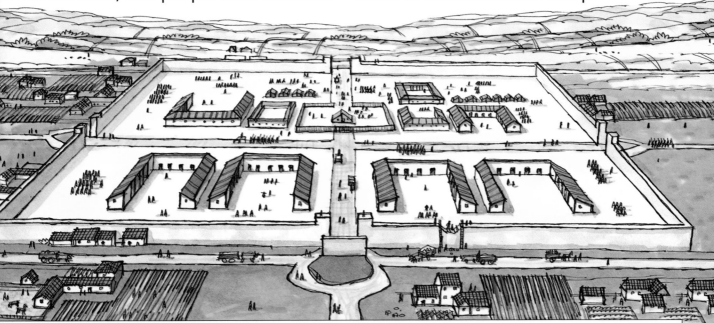

FIRING A CATAPULT

Today, Marcus is being taught how to fire a catapult. He and his friend, Maximus, wind down the catapult's huge beam, which has a sling at one end.

Then, a man known as a loader lifts a large, round stone and fits it into the sling. This stone can weigh as much as 30 kilos (about 66 pounds).

When the soldiers fire the catapult, the stone is flung high into the air and lands up to 30m (100ft) away. It can easily smash holes in the walls of enemy forts.

25

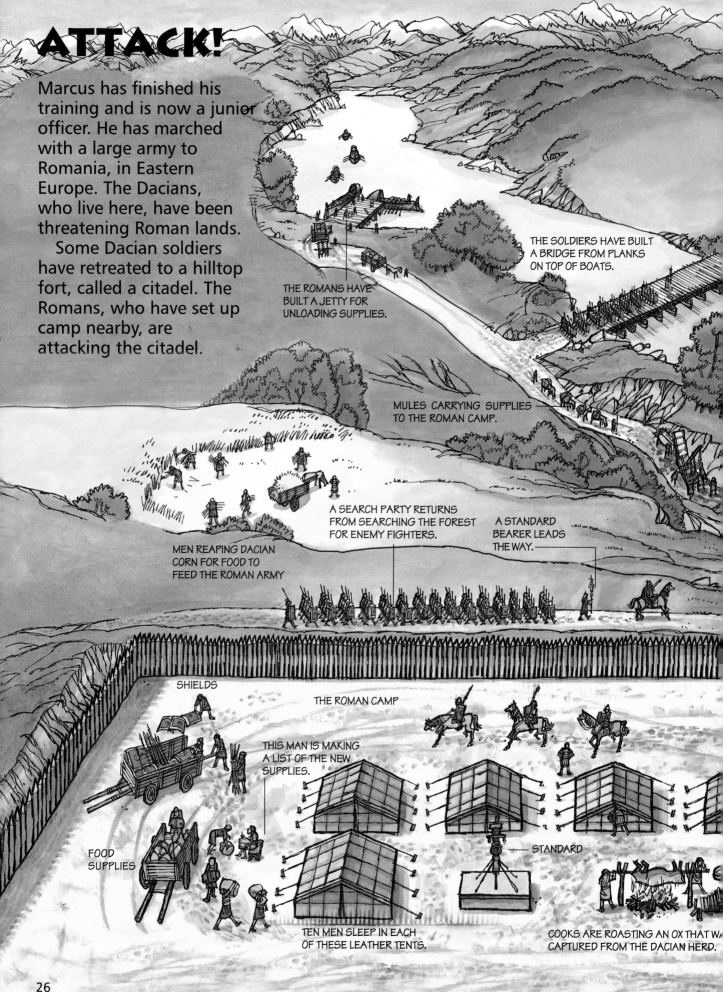

ATTACK!

Marcus has finished his training and is now a junior officer. He has marched with a large army to Romania, in Eastern Europe. The Dacians, who live here, have been threatening Roman lands.

Some Dacian soldiers have retreated to a hilltop fort, called a citadel. The Romans, who have set up camp nearby, are attacking the citadel.

THE SOLDIERS HAVE BUILT A BRIDGE FROM PLANKS ON TOP OF BOATS.

THE ROMANS HAVE BUILT A JETTY FOR UNLOADING SUPPLIES.

MULES CARRYING SUPPLIES TO THE ROMAN CAMP.

A SEARCH PARTY RETURNS FROM SEARCHING THE FOREST FOR ENEMY FIGHTERS.

A STANDARD BEARER LEADS THE WAY.

MEN REAPING DACIAN CORN FOR FOOD TO FEED THE ROMAN ARMY

SHIELDS

THE ROMAN CAMP

THIS MAN IS MAKING A LIST OF THE NEW SUPPLIES.

STANDARD

FOOD SUPPLIES

TEN MEN SLEEP IN EACH OF THESE LEATHER TENTS.

COOKS ARE ROASTING AN OX THAT WA CAPTURED FROM THE DACIAN HERD.

26

THE DACIAN VILLAGE IS ON FIRE.

THE DACIAN CITADEL

FLAMING MISSILES SET FIRE TO THE WALLS.

UNDER A TORTOISE OF SHIELDS, SOLDIERS APPROACH THE FORT.

CATAPULTS

THE ROMAN COMMANDER WATCHES THE ATTACK.

THESE HORSEMEN ARE FROM NORTH AFRICA. THEY HELP THE ROMANS BY ROUNDING UP DACIAN CATTLE.

MARCUS BRINGING A MESSAGE

PRISONERS

THESE DACIAN PRISONERS WILL BE SOLD AS SLAVES AFTER THE BATTLE.

OVENS

GUARDS

BAKERS ARE GRINDING WHEAT INTO FLOUR AND MAKING DOUGH.

WOUNDED SOLDIERS ARE LOOKED AFTER BY ARMY DOCTORS.

THE ROMAN EMPIRE

This map shows how the Roman empire looked a few years after your trip to Ancient Rome. It covered most of Europe and surrounded the Mediterranean Sea. All the areas shown in green on this map were part of the empire.

The map also shows what food and goods were brought to Rome and how they got there.

THE ROMANS BELIEVED THERE WERE TERRIBLE MONSTERS IN THE SEA.

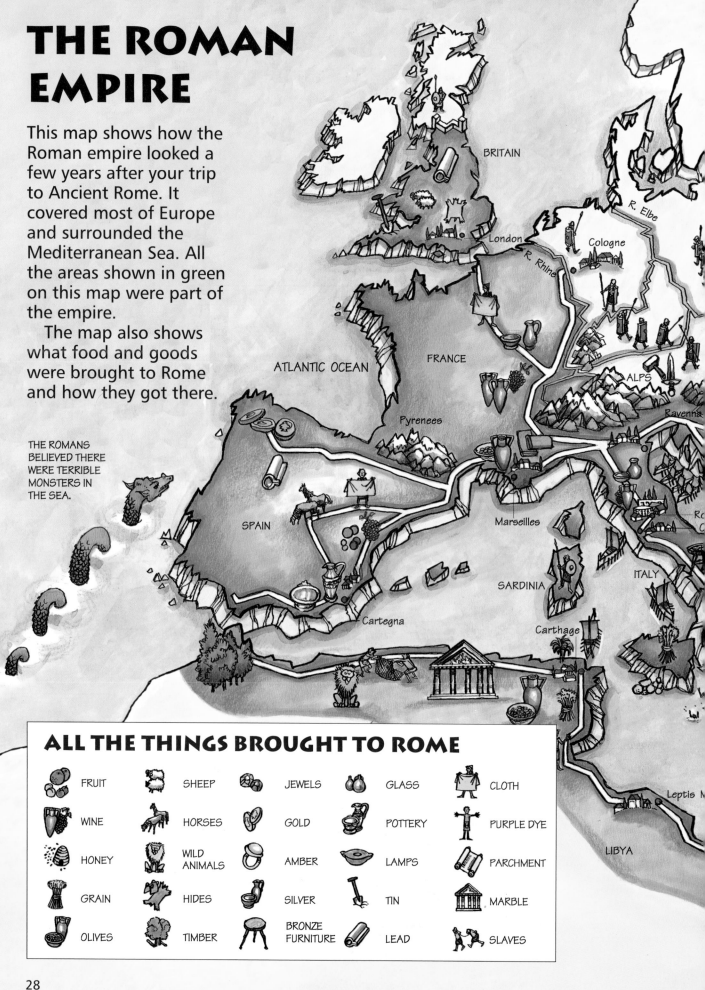

BRITAIN

R. Elbe

London

Cologne

R. Rhine

ATLANTIC OCEAN

FRANCE

ALPS

Pyrenees

Ravenna

SPAIN

Marseilles

ITALY

SARDINIA

Cartegna

Carthage

Leptis M

LIBYA

ALL THE THINGS BROUGHT TO ROME

FRUIT	SHEEP	JEWELS	GLASS	CLOTH
WINE	HORSES	GOLD	POTTERY	PURPLE DYE
HONEY	WILD ANIMALS	AMBER	LAMPS	PARCHMENT
GRAIN	HIDES	SILVER	TIN	MARBLE
OLIVES	TIMBER	BRONZE FURNITURE	LEAD	SLAVES

28

HE BARBARIANS INVADE

e Romans called the ople who lived outside eir empire "barbarians", aning foreigners. Some rbarians were wandering bes. They moved about, king for new land to farm and graze their animals. Sometimes they attacked Roman frontiers to reach the land inside the empire.

In the 4th century AD, thousands of barbarians invaded Roman lands from the northeast. They burned towns and cities, destroyed farms and killed people.

The empire gradually grew smaller. The Roman armies were driven back. The emperors couldn't get enough men or money to fight the invaders. In AD410, the barbarians captured Rome itself.

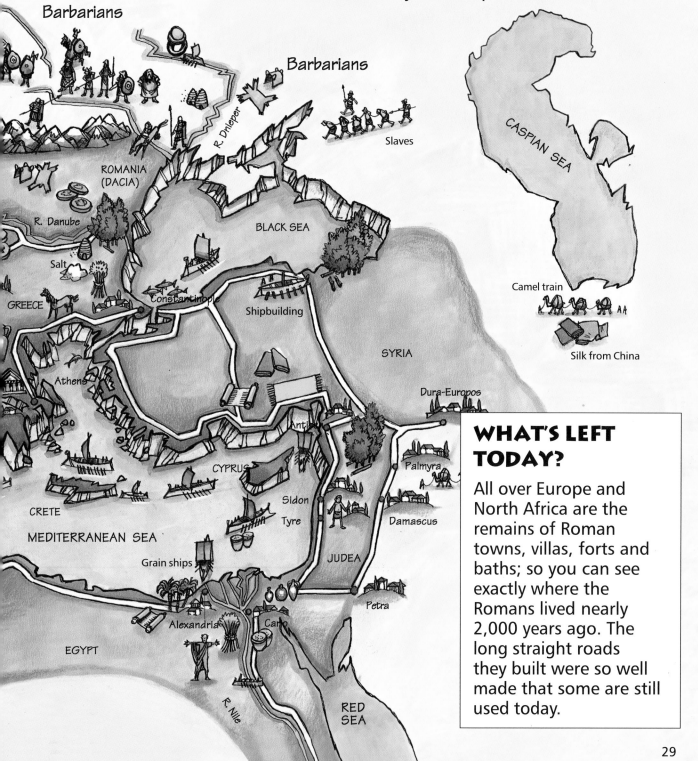

Barbarians

Barbarians

R. Dnieper

Slaves

CASPIAN SEA

ROMANIA (DACIA)

R. Danube

BLACK SEA

Salt

Camel train

GREECE

Constantinople

Shipbuilding

Silk from China

SYRIA

Athens

Dura-Europos

Antio

Palmyra

CYPRUS

Sidon

CRETE

Tyre

Damascus

MEDITERRANEAN SEA

JUDEA

Grain ships

Petra

Alexandria

Cairo

EGYPT

R. Nile

RED SEA

WHAT'S LEFT TODAY?

All over Europe and North Africa are the remains of Roman towns, villas, forts and baths; so you can see exactly where the Romans lived nearly 2,000 years ago. The long straight roads they built were so well made that some are still used today.

THE STORY OF ROME

In about 753BC (753 years before Jesus was born), a tribe from Northern Europe built a village on a hill near the Tiber River in Italy. They began to farm, and gradually the village grew into a city. Rome was ruled by kings.

SETTLING BY THE TIBER

In 509BC, the people decided they didn't want to be ruled by a king any more. Instead, every year they chose two men, called consuls, to rule. The Romans fought to protect their land, and captured more and more territory. By 250BC, they ruled the whole of Italy.

CONQUERING AN EMPIRE

In 206BC, war broke out with a sea-going people from Carthage, North Africa. The Romans built a huge fleet of ships and won great battles. The Carthaginians made a new base in Spain.

FIGHTING THE CARTHAGINIANS

A Carthaginian soldier named Hannibal gathered a huge army. Many of Rome's enemies joined him. They used elephants to cross over the Alps from Spain into Italy. Hannibal won many battles. But the Romans cut off his food supplies, so he couldn't reach Rome.

HANNIBAL'S ARMY

In 204BC, the Romans attacked Carthage. Hannibal sailed home to defend it, but he was defeated. Later, the Romans besieged the city and completely destroyed it. The people were killed or sold as slaves.

ATTACKING CARTHAGE

The Romans became the most powerful people in the Mediterranean. In Rome, the rich lived in great luxury. But many government officials became greedy and corrupt. The rulers of some areas of the empire demanded huge taxes from their subjects.

LIVING IN LUXURY

Civil war broke out in Rome when two generals tried to grab power. One marched his troops throu the streets, killing everyor he didn't like. In 73BC, a slave named Spartacus le a revolt. He escaped to Mount Vesuvius, joined b 90,000 slaves. He fought off the Roman army until he was killed in 71BC.

SPARTACUS AND HIS SLAVE ARMY

Two generals, Caesar an Pompey, struggled to control the government. Caesar marched from Ga to Rome, but Pompey left for Greece. Caesar defeat Pompey's army and Pomp escaped to Egypt, where was murdered. Caesar we to Egypt and helped Quee Cleopatra hold on to her throne. After more conque he returned to Rome.

In 45BC, Caesar becam sole ruler of Rome. He encouraged justice and planned to improve the c But his enemies feared he would try to become king, they murdered him in 44B

CAESAR'S MURDER

Caesar's heir, Octavian, defeated his rival Mark Antony in a sea battle. Antony and his wife, Cleopatra, killed themselves rather than face their defeat.

CLEOPATRA DYING

Octavian, Rome's first emperor, took the name Augustus. He strengthened the army and extended the empire. But he was defeated by German tribes. Throughout the empire, people built cities and roads. It was a time of peace and successful trade. Augustus was succeeded by members of his family. But an emperor wasn't like a king. Anyone who had enough support could come to power. For example, in one year there were four different emperors. Later, men who weren't even born in Rome became emperors. In AD117, a great general named Hadrian became emperor. He strengthened the frontiers and built a stone wall across northern Britain to keep out barbarian tribes. In Judea, the Roman army put down a revolt by the Jews and thousands were killed.

HADRIAN'S WALL

In the 2nd century AD the Roman empire reached its greatest extent. But the barbarians were attacking its frontiers. Southern German tribes attacked northern Italy. They were defeated, but still threatened the northern and eastern borders of the empire.

BARBARIANS ATTACK

In the 3rd century, the army dominated the government and chose emperors. The empire was too vast to control, and there were many civil wars. Old enemies, such as the Persians, began to regain land they had lost. Emperor Valerian was defeated and killed.

VALERIAN SUBMITS

People feared that Rome couldn't protect them from the barbarians. Soldiers posted across the empire spread new religions, such as Christianity. Emperors blamed the Christians for troubles in the empire, and put many Christians to death.

CHRISTIANS KILLED

In AD284, Diocletian, an army general, was declared emperor by his troops. He made the empire easier to control by dividing it into two halves, an eastern and western half. But there still wasn't enough money to pay the armies needed to fight off barbarian invaders.

Emperor Constantine made Christianity the state religion in AD320. He set up a new capital called Constantinople, from where he ruled the eastern half of the empire.

The barbarians invaded the western empire and destroyed Rome in AD410. They rapidly invaded the rest of Italy.

ROME IS RANSACKED

A barbarian became ruler of Italy in AD476. Constantinople held off its enemies until it was captured by Turks in AD1453.

Although the Roman empire was destroyed, the Romans have influenced many things in the modern world, including Western law and architecture. The languages now spoken in France, Spain, Portugal and Italy all developed from Latin – the Roman language. There are also many Latin words in Dutch, German and English.

INDEX

altar, 9
Antony, Mark, 31
aqueduct, 5, 15, 18-19
army,
   camps, 24-25, 26-27
   Dacian, 26-27
   Roman, 24-25, 26-27, 29, 30-31
   training, 24-25
   uniform, 24
Augustus, 31

bakers, 10, 12
   army, 27
barbarians, 29, 31
baths, 14-15
bread, 10, 12
building, 18-19

Caesar, 6, 30
Carthaginians, 30
catapults, 25, 27
chariot races, 11, 16, 17
cheese, 23
Circus, the, 17
citadel, 26
citizens, 3
Cleopatra, 30, 31
clothes, 9, 12
   cleaning, 13
Colosseum, the, 6, 16
Constantine, 31
Constantinople, 31
cooking, 13, 20-21
   army, 27

Dacians, 26-27
Diocletian, 31
drains, 8, 14

emperors, 6, 7, 30-31
empire, Roman, 6, 28-29, 30-31

farmers, 5, 22-23
feasts, 20-21
firemen, 6
food, 5, 12-13, 20-21, 22-23
forums, 6
fullers, 13

games, 16-17
   children's 10-11
gladiators, 16
grapes, 23

Hadrian, 31
Hannibal, 30
honey, 20, 21
horses, 17, 24
houses, 8-9, 18-19, 22, 25
hypocaust, 15

ink, 11

lamps, 10, 21
litters, 20
looms, 22

markets, 6, 13
masons, 19
meat, 13, 20, 21, 26
mosaics, 19
musicians, 13, 21

Octavian, 31
olive oil, 22, 23
olives, 21, 22, 23

pens, 11
pharmacists, 12
Pompey, 30
priests, 7

races,
   chariot, 17

children's 11
rivers,
   Tiber, 5, 30
roads, 4, 25, 29
Rome,
   baths, 14-15
   buildings, 6-7, 18-19
   shops, 12-13
   sports, 16-17
   story of, 30-31

Senate House, 7
schoolmasters, 10-11
schools, 3, 10-11
scrolls, 11
shops, 12-13
slaves, 3, 8-9, 10, 20-21, 27, 29
soldiers, 7, 24-25, 26-27, 29, 30-31
Spartacus, 31
spices, 20
staging posts, 5

taverns, 4
temples, 7
Tiber, River, 5, 30
togas, 9
tombstones, 4, 19
trade goods, 28-29

Valerian, 31
vegetables, 13, 20
villa, 22-23

water, 5,8, 14, 15, 18
weaving, 22
wheat, 12, 20, 22, 27
wine, 20, 21, 22
writing, 11

Additional illustrations on cover, pages 1 and 2 by Toni Goffe.

First published in 1976 and revised in 1997 by Usborne Publishing Ltd,
83-85 Saffron Hill, London EC1N 8RT, England.
Copyright © 1976, 1997 Usborne Publishing Ltd.
The name Usborne and the device 🎈 are Trade Marks of Usborne Publishing Ltd.
All rights reserved. No part of this publication may be reproduced, stored in a
retrieval system, or transmitted in any form or by any means, electronic,
mechanical, photocopying, recording or otherwise, without the prior
permission of the publisher. UE.
This edition first published in America in August 1997.
Printed in Belgium.